PUZZLE PIX

SPOT THE DIFFERENCE

CARLTON
KiDS

THE PICTURE CREDITS -THANKS!

The publishers would like to thank the following sources for their kind permission to reproduce the pictures in this book.

KEY: t=Top, b=Bottom, c=Centre, l=Left and r=Right

istockphoto.com: 86br, 87br, /Filonmar: 6–7, /Ismael Montero Verdu: 8–9, /Jerry McElroy: 10–11, /Owen Price: 12–13, /Charles Taylor: 14l, 15l, /Mark Evans: 14c, 15c, / Valerie Loiseleux: 14r, 15r, /Caroline Beecham: 16–17, /Michal Szota: 18–19, /Gina Luck: 20–21, /Rick Rhay: 22–23, /Philip Lange: 24–25, /Pederk: 26–27, /Lya Cattel: 28–29, /Fajean: 30–31, /Aleaimage: 32–33, /Merijn van der Vliet: 34–35, /Andrey Tsidvintsev: 36–37, /Mark Evans: 38–39, /Chris Pritchard: 40–41, /Anyka: 42–43, /Nautilus Shell Studios: 44–45, /Chris Crafter: 46–47, /Ricardo De Mattos: 48–49, /Afhunta: 50–51, /Elena Schweitzer: 52–53, /Zhan Tian: 54–55, /Craftvision: 56–57, /Андрей Савин: 58–59, /Elena Schweitzer: 60–61, /Dag Sjöstrand: 62–63, /Casey Hill: 64–65, /Amanda Rohde: 66–67, /Anthony Mayatt: 68–69, /Matthew Dixon: 70–71, /Mihail Glushkov: 72–73, /Hanhanpeggy: 74t, 75t, /Darrell Evans: 74bl, 75bl, /Igor Lubnevskiy: 74br, 75br, /Dmitry Bodrov: 76–77, /Zeynep Mufti: 78–79, /Tomasz Zachariasz: 80–81, /Benjamin Goode: 82–83, /Doug Cannell: 84–85, /Christian Reichenauer: 86tl, 87tl, /Kevin Thomas: 86tr, 87tr, /Frank van den Bergh: 86bl, 87bl, /Rob Belknap: 88–89

Every effort has been made to acknowledge correctly and contact the source and/or copyright holder of each picture and Carlton Books Limited apologises for any unintentional errors or omissions, which will be corrected in future editions of this book.

GET READY...

Calling all eagle eyes! How good are you at spotting differences? Throughout this book there are lots and lots of them. Your task is to find each one by comparing the picture on the left to the one on the right. Some of the differences are really easy to find, but others will drive you crazy! When you give up, which we're sure you will, you can find all the answers in the back of the book. For the few of you who do manage to find every single difference – congratulations! You can all give yourselves a Star Spotter Award!

PUZZLE 1
SWEET DREAMS

CAN YOU SPOT FIVE DIFFERENCES
BETWEEN THE TWO PICTURES?

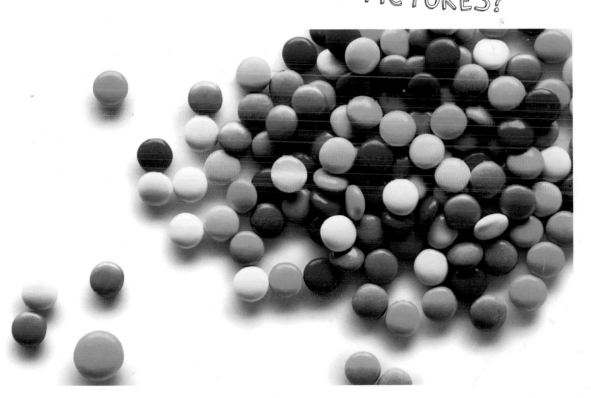

BOGGLING BUTTERFLIES

CAN YOU SPOT SEVEN DIFFERENCES BETWEEN THE TWO PICTURES?

UP, UP AND AWAY!

CAN YOU SPOT SIX DIFFERENCES BETWEEN THE TWO PICTURES?

A KNIGHT'S TALE

CAN YOU SPOT SEVEN DIFFERENCES BETWEEN THE TWO PICTURES?

PUZZLE 5
ROCKING ROBOTS

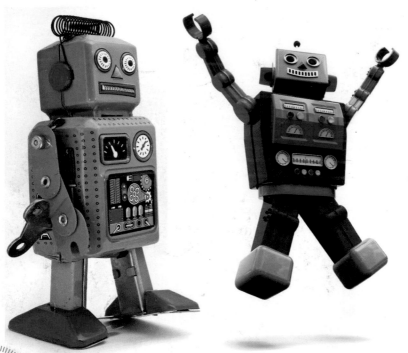

CAN YOU SPOT SEVEN DIFFERENCES BETWEEN THE TWO PICTURES?

ROLL UP, ROLL UP!

CAN YOU SPOT FIVE DIFFERENCES BETWEEN THE TWO PICTURES?

PUZZLE 7

ALL THE FUN OF THE FAIR

CAN YOU SPOT SEVEN DIFFERENCES BETWEEN THE TWO PICTURES?

CAN YOU SPOT FIVE DIFFERENCES BETWEEN THE TWO PICTURES?

PUZZLING PLAYGROUND

CAN YOU SPOT SIX DIFFERENCES BETWEEN THE TWO PICTURES?

PUZZLE 10

SANDY SPOT THE DIFFERENCE

CAN YOU SPOT SIX DIFFERENCES BETWEEN THE TWO PICTURES?

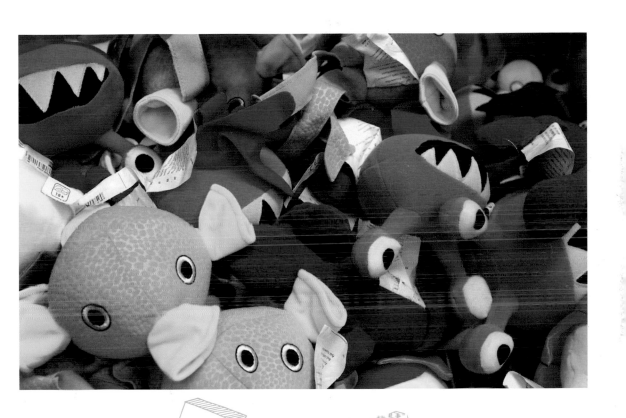

CAN YOU SPOT **SIX** DIFFERENCES BETWEEN THE TWO PICTURES?

PUZZLE 12 CROSS-TOWN TRAFFIC

CAN YOU SPOT SIX DIFFERENCES BETWEEN THE TWO PICTURES?

MIXED VEGETABLES

CAN YOU SPOT SEVEN DIFFERENCES BETWEEN THE TWO PICTURES?

CAN YOU SPOT SIX DIFFERENCES BETWEEN THE TWO PICTURES?

FAIRYTALE CASTLES

CAN YOU SPOT SIX DIFFERENCES BETWEEN THE TWO PICTURES?

FLYING HIGH. UP IN THE SKY

CAN YOU SPOT **FIVE** DIFFERENCES BETWEEN THE TWO PICTURES?

PUZZLE 17

FIRST OVER THE LINE

CAN YOU SPOT FIVE DIFFERENCES BETWEEN THE TWO PICTURES?

CAN YOU SPOT FIVE DIFFERENCES BETWEEN THE TWO PICTURES?

KNITTY KITTY

CAN YOU SPOT SIX DIFFERENCES BETWEEN THE TWO PICTURES?

GINGERBREAD HOME

CAN YOU SPOT SIX DIFFERENCES BETWEEN THE TWO PICTURES?

CAN YOU SPOT SEVEN DIFFERENCES BETWEEN THE TWO PICTURES?

ONE HUMP OR TWO?

CAN YOU SPOT **SIX** DIFFERENCES BETWEEN THE TWO PICTURES?

HERD OF HORSES

CAN YOU SPOT SIX DIFFERENCES BETWEEN THE TWO PICTURES?

CAN YOU SPOT SIX DIFFERENCES BETWEEN THE TWO PICTURES?

TAJ MAHAL MAGIC

CAN YOU SPOT **SIX** DIFFERENCES BETWEEN THE TWO PICTURES?

WHAT ARE YOU LOOKING AT?

CAN YOU SPOT SIX DIFFERENCES BETWEEN THE TWO PICTURES?

BRICK BONANZA!

CAN YOU SPOT **FIVE** DIFFERENCES BETWEEN THE TWO PICTURES?

CAN YOU SPOT SEVEN DIFFERENCES BETWEEN THE TWO PICTURES?

PUZZLE 29

SPOT THE STRIPES!

CAN YOU SPOT FIVE DIFFERENCES BETWEEN THE TWO PICTURES?

HARD-WORKING HOUND

CAN YOU SPOT FIVE DIFFERENCES BETWEEN THE TWO PICTURES?

CAN YOU SPOT **SIX** DIFFERENCES BETWEEN THE TWO PICTURES?

PROUD AS A PEACOCK

CAN YOU SPOT FIVE DIFFERENCES BETWEEN THE TWO PICTURES?

GONDOLA WONDER

CAN YOU SPOT **SIX** DIFFERENCES BETWEEN THE TWO PICTURES?

TECHNO TANGLE

CAN YOU SPOT SIX DIFFERENCES BETWEEN THE TWO PICTURES?

BOYS' TOYS

CAN YOU SPOT FIVE DIFFERENCES BETWEEN THE TWO PICTURES?

CAN YOU SPOT **SIX** DIFFERENCES BETWEEN THE TWO PICTURES?

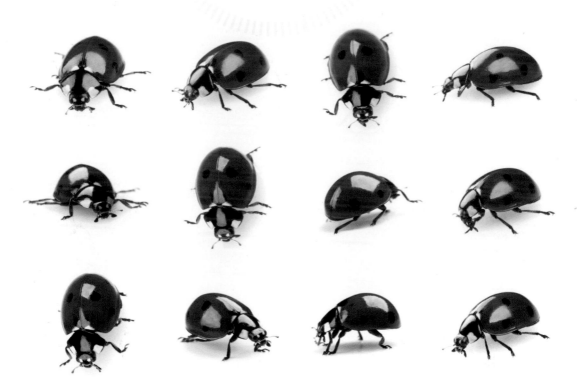

LUCKY LADYBIRDS

CAN YOU SPOT SIX DIFFERENCES BETWEEN THE TWO PICTURES?

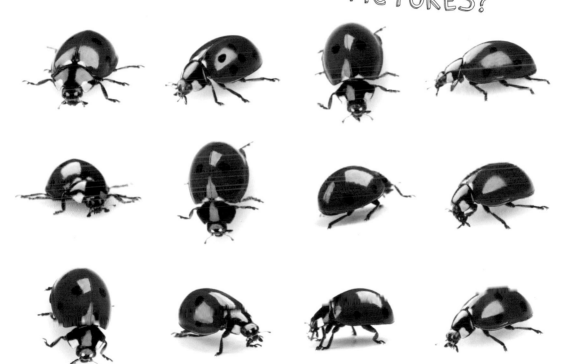

PUZZLE 39

PUZZLING PENGUINS

CAN YOU SPOT FIVE DIFFERENCES BETWEEN THE TWO PICTURES?

DIZZY DUCKIES

CAN YOU SPOT **SIX** DIFFERENCES BETWEEN THE TWO PICTURES?

WONDER WHEELS

CAN YOU SPOT FIVE DIFFERENCES BETWEEN THE TWO PICTURES?

MAGIC BEANS

89

THE ANSWERS!

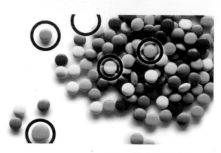

5
PUZZLE

6
PUZZLE

7
PUZZLE

8
PUZZLE

9
PUZZLE

10
PUZZLE

11
PUZZLE

12
PUZZLE

13

17

14

18

15

19

16

20

21
PUZZLE

25
PUZZLE

22
PUZZLE

26
PUZZLE

23
PUZZLE

27
PUZZLE

24
PUZZLE

28
PUZZLE

29
PUZZLE

33
PUZZLE

30
PUZZLE

34
PUZZLE

31
PUZZLE

35
PUZZLE

32
PUZZLE

36
PUZZLE